DRAGONFLY WHISPERER

Books by Steve K. Bertrand

The Silhouette of a Mallard's Wing
Where the Fly has Flown
Winter Chill
Chants of the Makah
On the Edge of Slumber
Don Quixote Give Up on Chivalry
The Little Book of Business Haiku
A Thousand Miles
Between the Tides
Tell Me, Moon
The Book of Fours
As The Crow Flies
To the Mountain's Peak
Into the Cavern
Warriors & Peacemakers
Dead Reckoning
Whispers from the Teahouse
At The Water's Edge
Where the River Flows
The Runner's Book of Haiku
Distant Islands
Paleolithica
Living Amongst the Sasquatch

Nonfiction

Mukilteo
Paine Field
Modern Everett

THE DRAGONFLY WHISPERER

Collected Haiku

STEVE K. BERTRAND

Copyright © 2019 by Steve K. Bertrand.

ISBN: Softcover   978-1-7960-5465-1
       eBook   978-1-7960-5464-4

All rights reserved. No part of this book may be reproduced or transmitted in any form or by any means, electronic or mechanical, including photocopying, recording, or by any information storage and retrieval system, without permission in writing from the copyright owner.

The views expressed in this work are solely those of the author and do not necessarily reflect the views of the publisher, and the publisher hereby disclaims any responsibility for them.

Any people depicted in stock imagery provided by Getty Images are models, and such images are being used for illustrative purposes only. Certain stock imagery © Getty Images.

Print information available on the last page.

Rev. date: 09/24/2019

To order additional copies of this book, contact:
Xlibris
1-888-795-4274
www.Xlibris.com
Orders@Xlibris.com
801043

For James Walker

"Whisper a wish to a dragonfly; and it will fly up to heaven and make it come true."

Preface

The Dragonfly Whisperer will tell you
all you need to know about dragonflies.
How they go way back in the fossil records,
300 million years,
& predate dinosaurs, that
during the Cretaceous period,
they were the size of hawks,
four wings & six legs,
but don't walk,
fierce predators of other insects,
like butterflies, mosquitoes & moths,
serrated teeth, the "toothed one".
They are gifted with incredible vision,
but cannot hear,
thirty thousand eyes within an eye,
life expectancy – but a year.
Five thousand species on the earth –
black petaltail, blue dasher, green darner,
red-veined darter.
To Native Americans, they symbolize
purity & happiness;
&, the key to coaxing dragonflies
onto your finger
is patience & those long-ago whispers
& sighs –
sun... water... meadow... wildflowers...
Those simple childhood joys.
Yes,
happiness attracts & lifts most dragonflies.

Steve K. Bertrand

Dragonfly whisperer –
coaxes dragonflies to tip
of his finger.

Late autumn –
snow geese flying low
above cat-tailed marsh...

Best beetle
live beneath damp log, than
eaten by starling.

Cranberry Lake -
Paddle-tailed Darner perched
on Salmonberry bush.

Talking on my cell phone,
crow –
listening...

And, after
the cherry's last blossom fell –
he died.

Her life –
too long staring down
a dry well.

And what of
the warrior, if there were
no wars?

First to break
the garden's soil –
peony.

Tossing crow
a piece of apple, he snatches it
& flies away...

After the snowmelt,
when river runs its purest –
she drinks.

Dog at the end
of my bed has fleas,
now – me.

So many people
on the sandy beach watching –
one ship.

So beautiful,
bullfrog's song, owl has stopped hooting
to listen…

Late August –
the jasmine-scented
night.

And, after
she died, the sea she loved –
ebbed & flowed...

I'm warning you –
don't pester crow;
he'll get even!

What will it be today,
hummingbird – Crocosmia
or nectar feeder?

The old man,
who mowed lawns in the neighborhood,
has died.

Mount Rainier,
tell me, how long till
you blow your top?

She is lonely:
& yet – turns away at
the slightest touch.

His old Army boots –
worn
when he works in the garden.

Her heart –
light as
the cricket's song.

Limb of apple tree
infested with caterpillars –
cut away.

Army backpacks
loaded with supplies for children
of poverty.

Ravenous –
the first bite of pizza
burns my mouth.

Rather than drop its leaves,
the maple
simply toppled over.

You & the sea,
love, both influenced by
the full moon.

Sweltering afternoon –
girls with a lemonade stand
in their front yard.

Dusk –
Strawberry Moon above
Mount Baker.

Some impressive art –
graffiti on
a passing train!

Your eyes, love –
How the carry the sparkle
of stars!

Local hardware store
flashing "OPEN"
at two in the morning.

So ends the old man's life –
wind plucks a leaf
from his apple tree.

When she is angry,
I drive to the beach – contemplate
calmness of sea.

Winter's coldness –
shot of whiskey
before bed.

Hiking –
Steller's jay perched atop
old lime kiln.

Waking this morning –
something has trampled
flowering tulips.

How determined those bees
to build a hive
beneath eaves of my house!

She jogs around
the lake with stroller, baby's head
bobbing...

Driving to work –
a deer trots across the road
in front of me...

Evening –
How I miss loon's song
on the old millpond.

Midnight,
coyote's howl – the neighbor's dog
answers.

Windstorm –
apples have toppled to ground
with tree.

When wind blows,
Civil War dead at Bull Run
whisper through the tall grass...

Braying mules,
I mistook as the ghosts
of Gettysburg.

Dawn –
Across the barren cornfield
trots coyote...

Overcast morning –
slug starts his journey
across sidewalk...

From atop the bookshelf,
cat
glares down at dog.

How well parakeet
imitates
husband's angry voice.

His stories
of a gloried youth –
outlast the truth.

My father's life –
never once,
the pronoun "I".

Turning 64 –
first time mom has forgotten
my birthday.

If you're going
to write every day, best keep
a sharp pencil.

Tide ebbs
& flows – sea shell upon
the sandy beach.

Fading off
to sleep –
crow's caw…

Some mornings,
she sits facing the sun, eyes closed,
sips her tea.

How amicably
jay & flicker share
my birdfeeder.

Dawn or dusk –
song birds
at their best!

Green husks,
brown silk – corn is ready
to harvest!

The dying cattails –
her
forgotten childhood.

Falling rain –
corner beggar man with
his empty cup.

Dusk –
Steller's jay lights by my pond
for a drink of water.

Above the ripened
cornstalks,
Harvest Moon.

Old frog
rests near edge of pond
where he once swam.

A woman
of Earth & Sky – she decorates
with feather baskets.

Such humility –
standing knee-deep
in the ocean.

Old mill site –
gray heron on decayed piling
fishing...

Coming down
the dirt road – old man in nothing
but faded blue jeans.

Shadow Darner
hovering above lily pads
on koi pond...

The old man said –
"Cultivate your spirit.
That's religion enough."

That auto mechanic
left his cigar smells
in my car.

Night before battle –
long talks by the fire,
late into night.

After 22 years,
the neighbors have moved –
how dark their house.

Our fast-paced culture –
Was there really once a world
older than now?

He rarely spoke;
but when he did – his words
carried water.

Wild boy –
abandoned in the woods,
raised by wolves.

That Native basket,
has a horse motif –
tails down.

Nights,
Makah fishermen dance around the fire
in Moon masks.

Tell me,
Is not Wild Woman
also Bigfoot?

He said –
"I didn't ask to be a poet;
words just come."

Ah, to be as carefree
as those
gently passing clouds.

At the stoplight,
tank top gal in Dodge Ram,
country music blaring...

Night –
She thinks of her dead husband,
turns her face to moon.

August morning –
red dragonfly skirts above
koi pond...

Youth –
to sleep in a haystack,
count falling stars...

Rain has driven all
but pigeons
from the park.

While Notre Dame burns,
mourners sing –
"Ave Maria"...

Trying to capture words
for this poem, butterfly flits
through my yard...

She places
jay's feather in a Native basket
for good luck.

Late summer –
laden apple tree
thins itself.

Far off –
a passing ship
at sea.

How free,
the blind, from trappings
of the material world.

July –
new driver learning her school
bus route.

In the town square,
an old man
& his guitar.

As she marries
husband number ten, still –
she blames it on the men.

That homeless man –
his whole world
in a shopping cart.

Spring evening –
pink sky, blue sky,
pink sun, blue moon.

Street lamp –
illuminating the amber-leafed
maple tree.

In the park,
crow contemplating
a heroin needle...

She said,
"I'm giving up all things nice,
including you."

Old woman –
spends her days watching birds
in the backyard.

Sidewalk beggar man –
sharpens his wooden spear
with a pocket knife.

He spent his life
acquiring wisdom no one
listened to.

So many apples
knocked down
by last night's rain.

Dawn –
pink & blue-streaked sky
above white Cascades.

A week of rain,
& crow,
in no mood for singing.

Calling my wife,
the neighbor dog
responds.

Saturday morning –
teapot whistling,
parakeet chirping...

Often, if I'm patient,
the poem
comes to me.

Old rotary phone
rings, but –
no one answers.

Boy Scout Boot Camp –
a 25-mile hike,
three farts.

Old crow
still carries a bit
of his youthful strut.

His graffiti,
anywhere else but my fence –
art.

After the rain,
robin happily splashing
in a mud puddle!

Why such
a long face last night,
moon?

August afternoon –
sunlight dances on blue dragonfly's
wings.

Driving Highway 2 –
a semi-truck nose-deep
in a grassy pasture.

Suddenly,
loon pops above surface
of cat-tailed lake.

Country farm –
gray cloud resting atop
tall haystack.

Gravenstein apples –
more on the ground
than tree.

Pulling weeds –
bee chases me away from
blooming lavender.

Not a good idea,
slug, basking in the bright
sunshine.

Desert trek –
the old man
& his fishing pole.

Above the Dvorak
orchestra on the radio –
screeching crows.

Far as the eye
can see – green & yellow
dandelion field.

The old man said,
"Sometimes I go to the park
just to watch children play."

Three wooden posts
in a farmer's field, each occupied
by a crow.

Evening –
yellow tractor rests atop
a pile of dirt.

That charge at Gettysburg –
some did not outrun
the bugle's call.

That Raven,
carries Blood Moon
in his right eye.

Fire dying,
shot of whiskey to keep away
winter's chill.

Tell me,
woman, how many moons
since you last smiled?

After the windstorm,
toppled
stone cairn.

Driving past the baseball field
where I spent my childhood –
cricket match.

Old brick garage –
blackberry & yellow yarrow,
thrush's nest.

Something toppled
my tallest sunflower
around midnight.

Jogging down the street,
neighbor gal hollers – "You can run
through my sprinkler!"

From childhood,
grandpa's voice whispering
through weeping willow...

In the garden,
Morning glory is first
to greet me.

Looking down
on the neighbor's house –
moss atop the roof.

Moving a stone
in the garden – out crawls
black beetle.

Between mainland
& island – tug pulling barge
of sawdust.

She said,
"Leave beach shells
on the beach!"

The wooden dock
of childhood – where we waited
for catfish.

My childhood,
three words – baseball, pirates,
dinosaurs.

Baby's vomit –
on the head of the bronze
heron statue.

Cradling hot coffee,
watching sunrise
above Cascade Mountains...

Almost every home
in Ireland – picture of
John F. Kennedy.

The lonely poet –
nothing left
but his words.

Snow falling –
homeless man huddled beneath
tarp & shopping cart.

At the bottom
of the birdbath –
dead slug.

Always –
eagle perched in his fir snag
by the bay.

Atop seawall,
crow lands with his morsel
of food.

Dusk –
slug makes his way along sidewalk
toward variegated hosta.

The leash
controls both dog
& man.

Vet in wheelchair
motors through bikini barista
latte stand.

My life with you
uncertain, wife, but moon –
constant.

Red-tailed hawk,
circles, then lands, atop
dead, fir snag.

Returning
from vacation, birds have eaten
my blueberries!

Daybreak –
wind blows, crow flies
cawing...

Let me run
just fast enough to
slow down time.

Heat wave –
bird
feathers everywhere.

Yard work –
battle victories, but
never the war.

The jagged,
snow-capped peak where
mountain goats play.

4:30 –
ever so slowly dawn
approaching...

Sunrise –
glacier & wildflowers blanket
east side of mountain.

Every morning,
a walk with her dog
& mocha.

She was a feisty,
little girl, a stick against
the wind.

Every night,
my dog on time for dinner
& - no watch.

Green light,
but the truck in front of me
waits on a pigeon.

Three short & a long knock –
Is that fate
knocking on my door?

Butterfly bush flowering,
Crocosmia
decides it will too.

Who needs
an alarm clock with crow
outside my window.

Monday morning –
rumble of garbage truck
through neighborhood.

So many great
baseball cards lost in the spokes
of bicycle tires.

In time,
the weight of the material world
crushed her.

That squeaky-clean
blonde in faded green tank top
& dirty blue jeans.

That boy,
flirting with a girl, & little sister
tagging along.

Summer afternoon –
old man unleashes his dog
in the meadow.

Old eagle –
ruffled feathers, but how proud
he holds his head!

That man –
running out of body parts
to tattoo.

When the pace of life
is slow – you notice snail
on the sidewalk.

Jogging down
the highway – wooden cross
& wilted flowers.

Sometimes, right out
of the cracks in a sidewalk –
poetry emerges.

Winter morning –
boom, boom, boom of waves
against beach...

Dead calm –
how perfect the bay
for skipping rocks.

After the rain,
how high flickering flames
of bonfire.

Nice surprise –
a women's yoga class
at the beach!

Ancient wilderness –
craggy peaks, Douglas fir,
billowy clouds, blue sky.

My coach said,
"Focus on your race; don't worry
about the ticking clock."

Driving to town –
chipmunk scurries across
the street...

At the edge
of forest, black-tailed deer
nibbling ferns.

You can't do a Rain Dance,
then –
complain about the rain.

She walked
only as far as the tide
ran out.

Low tide
& sandy beach littered
with golf balls.

She had a habit
of stopping
before she got there.

At a stoplight,
little heads bobbing from back seat
of car in front of me.

After a day
of yard work, I wash
my garden hands.

School's end –
kids in the neighborhood head
to the sandlot.

Strolling through town –
an Oreo cookie
on the sidewalk.

Morning of a marathon,
most important thing –
bathroom stop.

Spring afternoon –
two crows play chase above
the ball field.

How lovely,
the neighbor's yard,
lavender in bloom.

Spring afternoon –
hawk glides gently above
the meadow...

Sighing, he said –
"Ah, the mountains
in our lives."

That long mountain hike –
how open
we were to talking.

He said,
"I shy away from groups; prefer
to talk one-on-one."

Two sides
to a mountain – light
& dark.

A slight breeze
on a spring day – dandelion
spores...

Strolling the river bank –
a pocketful
of river rocks.

And in the end,
the path traveled –
we do so alone.

Ripening blueberries –
some for me,
some for the birds.

Where is the crow
to whom this withered, fallen
feather belongs?

Maybe it's silly,
my three favorite flowers –
iris, orchid, lily.

She said,
"We've become Orpheus & Eurydice.
I'll not follow you to hell!"

Sniffing evening air –
somewhere in the distance,
rain coming...

Out of nowhere,
bird shit
on my windshield!

Dawn –
two rabbits scamper across
my backyard lawn...

Old man driving –
such a worried look
upon his face.

Halfway through the gala event,
I notice –
my socks don't match.

Just last week,
a wallet full of money,
this week – empty.

Commute gridlock –
gray gulls on a lamp-post
laughing...

Pollution
& – the Dead Sea deader than
it already is.

Muddy stretch of trail –
I tip-toe across fallen Western
red cedar.

With wind
at its back, how hard waves rush
rocky beach.

That woman
walking towards Nordstroms –
such determination!

Spring morning –
ducks resting on bank
of old mill pond.

Why just yesterday,
the blue iris
in full bloom.

In the garden,
everywhere I don't want it growing –
Foxglove.

That BIG truck –
how he bulls his way
through traffic!

Every time I turn around,
another weed
in the garden!

Old fisherman –
pile of cigarette butts
at the bottom of his boat.

Winter night –
wisp of cloud beneath
pale, full moon.

Slowly rotting away –
abandoned barn
in the farmer's field.

High up
in a leafless tree –
bird's nest.

Full worm moon –
robins in the garden
pulling up worms.

He said,
"I live my life without paying
attention to time."

Smart fly,
open door, heads outside,
my first try.

Autumn
& – are not the forest colors
painting enough?

Evening breeze –
jasmine trellis
trembles...

Forest path,
wooden foot bridge,
dry creek bed.

How happy
the homeless man who found
a quarter on the sidewalk!

Strong wind & rain –
we trudge through town
toward the tavern.

She was in her prime,
& -
all the boys noticed.

A slight breeze –
how easily gulls ride
rolling sea...

It seems like
just yesterday – our laughter
from the old sandlot.

Turns out
his soul mate –
wasn't.

Tending garden
on a sweltering day, drink from garden hose –
enough.

Spring morning –
robin on split-rail fence
in full-throated song.

I call to
winter warbler, but his thoughts
are on spring.

Wings atwitter,
gray gull riding a current
of wind.

Those birds
heading into the wind are getting
nowhere.

Up the mountain,
an old man goes humming
yesterday's song.

Those three
bird nests in that aged oak –
condos?

Some trees
more excited about coming spring
than others.

Long since abandoned,
this farm – manure pile has lost
its smell.

Winter morning –
I drive through grayness
toward Mount Baker...

All my life –
boats sailing north/south,
trains running east/west.

Grandma's Irish
cough syrup – clove, honey,
lemon, whiskey.

Posted from the bridge
where we used to jump – "No jumping/diving
from bridge".

That bi-plane –
a relic from
the by-gone days.

Windstorm –
how tightly White-faced Meadowhawk
clings to alder twig.

Look –
In the red & yellow tulip field,
Trumpeter swans!

Dawn –
otter slowly swims up
Ebey Slough...

Where old mill stood
at mouth of Snohomish River –
wood pilings.

Autumn afternoon –
heron fishing from a drifting snag
on Steamboat Slough.

Just ghost tracks
where the Everett & Monte Cristo Railway
once ran.

Early spring –
brown bear fishing from edge
of Stillaguamish River.

Dusk –
Great blue heron lifts
off the marsh...

Low tide –
sea birds wading into
the shallows.

That first kiss
by the lake – moon, stars
& frog song...

Overgrown field –
where the farmer's abandoned tractor
rests.

Old sandlot –
abandoned but for a murder
of crows.

That boy & girl –
all afternoon to carve their names
in dry cliff-side.

April
& every four days – lawn
needs mowing.

He grabs two
fortune cookies, in case the first one
isn't good enough.

Silly to the point
of ridiculous – that
teenage girl.

Dangling his feet
into nothingness – that boy
on the bridge rail.

Nightfall –
firefly skirts rooftop
of neighbor's house.

Spring –
jasmine vine reaching for limb
of weeping cedar.

Tag end
of October & - the weather
holding fine.

Saturday morning –
"Spring's coming! Spring's coming!"
sing the birds.

A coelacanth slowly crawls
from sea to land –
she glances at me.

Low tide –
boat fenders marooned
on sandy beach.

Deep beneath
layers of earth – man's
accumulated guilt.

Gazing at Wolf Moon,
this thought –
"Are we not all astronauts?"

Winter morning –
the warmth of a porcelain
tea cup.

Because he didn't know
what else to do –
he wrote.

August afternoon –
two Goldfinches
at my Niger thistle feeder.

My life –
constant ebb & flow
of sea.

Long time
on the vine, & yet, jasmine –
how pungent!

New neighbors –
they've brought a bird feeder
& cat.

From a distance,
deer silently eye apples
on my tree.

Sometimes I climb
the apple tree just to show
I still can!

At the beach,
my grandson pokes a seal carcass
with a stick.

Spring –
ducks return to my pond
with friends.

Gray, wet, cold,
the Northwest, & yet – palm tree
in the neighbor's front yard!

There goes my childhood –
on the wings
of a butterfly...

When she jogs –
the whole world knows
her agony!

New BB gun –
boy eyes birds a bit
differently.

She loves
her butterfly bush; & –
so do butterflies!

The mighty oak has died;
& still –
birds flock to its limbs.

Grandma
has passed; but – her presence felt
in the garden.

Gradually,
Salish Sea nibbles away
at Hat Island...

Such blind persistence –
fly refusing
to leave my house.

Gazing upon tulips
all afternoon,
I dream of tulips that night.

Man kills sea lions
eating salmon; so he can eat
the salmon himself.

Spring evening –
gardening to
the robin's song.

Lucky you,
dragonfly, rescued by child
from spider's web.

He never worried
about insurance till his house
burned down.

All my life –
people passing in & out
of shadows.

I could let
her go; but for the memory
of Cancun.

Shouting at you,
love, above the river's
roar...

Sometimes I find
I'm more myself at dusk
than dawn.

How worn
wooden ladle that rests beside
the stone well.

As if hiking
this mountain weren't enough –
cherry blossoms too!

Ramadan –
toast & tea before
the dawn.

I call my cat
& - the neighbor's dog
comes running.

Looking in the mirror –
Do I see the same person
other people see?

Old man
in the park – how easily he laughs
all by himself.

Fruit stand –
an old woman samples
the Bing cherries.

Old salamander
at bottom of my pond – when did you
last see the sun?

At the end of the earth,
how easily stars
tumble into the sea.

How the damselfly
loves
to hover!

Low tide –
gray heron wades amongst
the seagrass...

Not a bird of prey,
but heron –
predatory.

Between Gedney,
Whidbey & Camano Islands –
sailboat passing...

A little girl
excitedly yells "dolphin",
points at a seal pup.

Hovering between
blue sea & blue sky –
blue dragonfly.

Grandpa's house –
waking to the smell of bacon,
eggs & toast.

Local market –
yellow butterfly inspects
the fresh produce.

Kicking off his sandals,
crow struts along
sandy beach.

Passing ship –
kayaker braces for the
approaching wake…

Odd –
eagle's perch without
the eagle.

When frustrated –
she changes her point of view
rather than hairstyle.

In his dreams,
grandpa skipper of the Black Prince
once again.

Jogging –
how the woman struggles,
but not her dog.

Though an occasional cloud,
nothing more trustworthy
than sun & moon.

Maple dresses
for three seasons; Douglas fir
for four.

By the side
of the road, patch
of yellow yarrow.

A smile upon
my father's face just mentioning –
"fishing".

Above the August creek,
Four-spotted Skimmer dragonfly
glides...

Low tide –
boy on sandy spit gathering
golf balls.

Abandoned railroad bed –
a garden
of wildflowers.

Side of the road –
woman in a bike helmet
picking blackberries.

After gardening,
washing the toil
from my hands.

Gull rises
from beach – drops a clam shell
against the rocks.

Dead calm –
a sailboat silently motors northward
on Possession Sound...

For lovers,
troubadours announce the
approaching dawn.

Walking through the garden,
thorny rose
grabs hold & won't let go!

Circling above
the country church –
red-tailed hawk...

That pottery teacher
in junior high school – taught us to make
ashtrays.

Is it true –
the Marlboro Man died
from cancer?

Blueberries left to the birds,
since
the old man died.

Strange to see
eagle & crow perched on
the same fir limb.

Abandoned homestead
& its ripened
field of barley.

Outdoor café closed;
but for
the gathered crows.

July –
by the Nooksack River,
corn shoulder-high.

Election year –
speedway lined with
campaign signs.

With each hurt,
she shed her skin
like an onion.

He almost died
upon that mountain – spent his days
coming back to life.

Interesting –
those eagles gathered atop the farmer's
manure pile.

I-5 traffic slowing –
two deer
near edge of freeway.

Hawk
in an endless blue sky
& - all day to fly.

Westward ho,
& - Where did all
the Indians go?

The mountain
that almost claimed his life –
he still visits.

That smoothie –
looks green,
tastes raspberry!

Dusk –
owl's lullaby from limb
of Mountain hemlock...

Because children
run through the sprinkler,
dog does too!

Before nightfall,
Steller's jay's scolding
while I garden.

Emerging from permafrost,
the ancient
mammoth tusk.

Going down
to the sea, always –
my spirit returns.

A thousand years,
still,
the same wish – peace.

Dawn –
to the east,
mist in the valley.

A week ago,
the heavy snows, & now –
record-breaking sun!

Rather than bird-watching,
she spent her days
crunching numbers.

That writer –
so good with letters,
so poor with numbers.

Sometimes on summer days,
she sings
for no reason at all.

Evening –
rising from a golden wheatfield,
flutter of sparrows.

August evening –
golden fields, red barn,
thunder clouds.

How hard
that crow flaps his wings
against the wind.

So dilapidated
the old barn – even the ghosts
have fled.

After the rain,
crows scavenging amongst
the horse pasture.

Hour wait
at the Canadian border – she pulls out
her knitting.

That girl
with the flowered tattoo running
down her neck – hmmm.

Driving through Canada,
everywhere –
"Merge like a zipper".

Gradually,
"Wine, women & song" became –
"Sex, drugs, rock-&-roll".

Running the woodland trail,
I happen upon
a forest cairn.

Where yesterday a patch
of forest snow,
today – sun.

Black Petaltail –
so you too are drawn
to cherry blossoms!

Lavender blooming
& suddenly –
bumblebees are here!

Low tide –
purple starfish upon
a seagrass beach.

Such a diverse
colony – egrets, herons
& cormorants.

Best view
of the football game – egret nest
atop stadium lights.

I-5 –
blonde girl in passenger seat,
bare feet on dashboard.

Hovering in the distance –
helicopter
or large dragonfly?

Grandpa said,
"Pick only the bluest blueberries.
White & green won't ripen."

Between you & I,
dragonfly – I don't think
you're the devil.

Skateboard kid –
bandages on knees & elbows
& no helmet.

Digging for clams –
an ancient
dinosaur bone!

Just walking her dog,
neighbor lady attracts
a gaggle of children.

How like my boss,
that crow,
inspecting my garden work.

To the north –
yellow & red tulip fields
blooming...

When troubled,
she worked it out
in the kitchen.

She said,
"The less I think,
the less the ink."

Setting sun –
swallowed by the distant
mountains.

Is not full moon
lantern light enough to steer
the boat by?

In the air,
promising of impending
weather.

The dog's ears
raised toward thunder
in the distance.

Gust of wind,
separates leaves on the tree –
dead from dying.

Ancient roots
pushing the sidewalk up
at odd angles.

That little boy lost –
still chasing butterflies through
summer meadows?

Hundreds of ripe cherries
on the tree, & - crow has eaten
all but three.

The babbling brook
seems
happiest come spring!

The old lime kiln
where deer come to nibble
on its mossy sides.

On his death bed,
the old man's last words –
"Good night".

Every once in a while,
on a summer breeze – childhood
memories…

She does
her best humming while
dishwashing.

The old church
burned down; they blamed it on
a firefly.

Tell me,
Mount Baker, will you ever
awaken?

Her stories
about growing up – better than
the truth.

Spring –
out of the birdhouse
ventures spider.

Every night,
mother's words – "I love you.
Did you brush your teeth?"

In the old pond,
an old frog sings
his old song.

How familiar
those two have become beneath
blossoming cherry.

Flowering peony –
as beautiful at dusk
as dawn.

In the park,
how silently bare trees carry
their winter burdens.

On the Island of Dragonflies,
such
happiness abounds!

An M.B.A. –
She was looking for someone to manage,
not marry.

All afternoon,
old man sits amongst bunch grass,
tosses stones into sea...

Spring
& the only thing awake
in the garden – peonies.

To the edge
of my koi pond, robin brings
his song...

She said,
"What should we do now;
my cell phone's dead?"

So long heron
has studied this river –
I bet he could draw it!

He died in peace;
quite different than how
he lived his life.

What draws bear
to river
draws eagle too.

Gramps –
"Old age doesn't just happen;
it sneaks up on you."

The eagle
is long gone; but –
his nest remains.

The old priest –
his sins hidden beneath
a black robe.

She said,
"Less 'me',
more 'we'."

Old frog
from his old pond
gazes upon – new moon.

Autumn –
raked into a pile
in the neighbor's front yard.

For decades after the battle,
whispers
from the tall grass...

Slowly,
Morning glory sneaks toward
unsuspecting daisies...

That book –
dog-eared from
a dog's chewing.

Caw... Caw... Caw...
crow's good morning & good night
song too.

Caught in a sudden rain –
she
should have worn a bra.

The Great blue heron
exudes
his greatness!

Bright stars,
brighter moon – the sea
a sparkle.

Upon the sandy beach,
stones
polished by the sea.

Auto accident –
She said, "I'm the one at fault."
then, took it back.

Driving my truck –
I swerve to miss a squirrel,
run into a tree.

Waiting –
little sister for big sister
to come home from school...

He sold
the pickup he swore
he'd never sell.

At the edge
of the sea, she offers her prayer
for the orcas.

Such gratitude
expressed from the little,
rescue dog!

Sun setting
beyond tree line, hoot owl –
hooting...

How sad
old frog since moving
to his new home.

This old house –
moaning roof, creaking steps,
rattling pipes.

Not quite spring,
& yet – song
of the House sparrow...

While backyard birds
peck at my feeders – I mow
the front lawn.

The pond
has dried up – old frog too tired
to move.

She applies
her morning make-up as if
it were a painting.

The Skeleton Flower's petals –
transparent
in the falling rain.

Dawn,
old Ford pickup at stoplight –
pop-eye.

He wasn't the type
to stand by the cracker barrel
in idle chit-chat.

Spring,
waking this morning –
hoot of an owl...

Dawn –
the old farmer's stubble
of cornfield.

When I'm feeling down,
music
lifts me up!

The blooming
Crocosmia Lucifer – how the hummingbirds
hover!

Strolling the beach –
I go
where the poem takes me...

August
& still – my strawberries rewarding me
with delicious fruit!

Watching the otters play –
I think upon
my childhood.

August evening –
an Irish setter trots along
the sandy beach...

Here in the country –
just flowers, firewood & honey
for sale.

Dusk –
bare foot romantics stroll
the sandy beach...

I find myself hollering
at a jackrabbit –
"Get out of the road!"

Watering house plants –
a trail of water
from the leaky can.

He loved birds;
but –
his BB gun more.

How clear
the peel of church bells
on winter mornings.

The wild rabbit,
who used to scamper away,
doesn't anymore.

What am I to think
of the sparrow
who begs at my table?

Dead Douglas fir snag –
where the
old eagle perches.

How purple iris
brightens the koi pond
each spring!

The ripe squash –
nibbled upon
by a night critter.

Planting flowers –
spider climbs up the pot
for a better view.

We said
our "helloes" & "good-byes"
to cherry blossoms.

Will you turn
your back on me too,
pale moon?

Wild birds,
so loyal, as long as
the feeders full.

The new neighbors –
already talking
about a fence.

Teenage girl,
standing in the sea – how strong
the pull of tide.

That stray cat,
we got for free,
"Lost - $100 Reward".

Rain has begun
to fall upon our picnic –
crow's laughter...

The evening cool
such a welcome relief
from the heat!

Tell me again –
How did the peasant
come by his humility?

Spring afternoon –
maples
dancing in the wind…

Neighbor horse,
who ate the grass in my back yard –
has started on the front.

How stubborn
that fly who won't shoo
outside.

That girl
riding her bike in the rain –
smiling…

Waking this morning –
sunflower
peeks in my window...

The railroad
hasn't run for years; but – its whistle
still in the trees.

Yesterday's poem
rewritten – a new poem
emerges.

Decided,
then undecided – ebb & flow
of sea...

That picnic,
carefully planned for everything,
but – rain.

We never see
the neighbor lady, except to get
her mail.

Pike Place Market –
red dragonfly lights upon
the honeysuckle.

Boy waiting
for grandpa to make it through
the crosswalk…

Is not the trunk
of mighty oak its mind;
& limbs – its thoughts?

Sometimes she sits
upon the beach just to feel the sand
between her toes.

Miles of sandy beach –
a man releases his dog
from leash.

Mist lifting from islands,
calm sea,
Nordic tug heading northward...

Eight-Spotted skimmer –
how pale yellow
your face.

From out of nowhere,
waves begin rolling in
upon the beach...

"The fishing is no good here."
says heron
lifting off the bay.

After the storm,
to the beach –
beachcombers.

Low tide –
rocks, seaweed, driftwood,
sea grass, clam shells.

Dead calm –
sea birds skirt inches above
the bay...

Gazing at Hat Island,
I wonder – "Do they ever gaze
toward the mainland?"

That piece of driftwood
in the sea,
I mistook for a seal.

August morning –
how content gulls to simply drift
upon the sea...

Dusk approaching –
last ray of sunlight shining
on Whidbey Island.

Roses blooming,
mother on the front porch
waving good-bye...

The gardener said,
"Stand beneath Umbrella cherry
& prune outward."

Netting leaves
from koi pond – I save
a bumblebee!

That girl –
noticed wherever
she goes.

August morning –
rabbit nibbles on windfall apple
by road.

Possession Sound –
an orca slaps
its dorsal fin.

Autumn –
gray squirrel at the end
of a cherry limb.

Nightfall –
gathered wolves in a dark circle
of forest.

Tonight –
such a fat & sassy moon
in the sky.

Autumn evening –
low clouds
thick with rain.

By interstate –
ragged panhandler with
sodden handmade sign.

Waitress at café —
blue hair, blue calf tattoo,
blue mood.

Scrolling through my
phone contacts –
a few deceased.

Smiling –
stone Buddha waist high
in Mondo grass.

Green Lake –
wading pool full of
laughing children.

Walking the beach –
crow's feather stuck
in the sand.

August morning –
gardener pruning the neighbor's
yellow roses.

The neighbor
walking her dog –
no poop bag.

The neighbor died –
long line of cars & trucks
outside their house.

Smiles on the face
of the girl
holding a sunflower.

Young woman –
texting her way through
the market…

Is it instinctual –
dogs
& fire hydrants?

That girl –
pink fingernails to go with
her pink Volkswagen.

That flute player –
boy can he
tootle a tune!

Something about the ocean,
salt breeze –
decay & renewal.

How long & thin
clouds
pulled by the wind.

As they drift
across the sky, shards of sunlight
light the tops of clouds.

She said,
"Can you enjoy things without
possessing them?"

The winter garden,
her garden –
blanketed with snow.

Low tide,
stranded driftwood –
three gray gulls.

Late summer –
neighbor lady watering
her dahlias.

Somewhere deep inside her,
the music
she longed to play.

Indian names,
tell me – who takes the land
but keeps their names?

Those words in anger
spoken to her – how I wish
I'd swallowed stones.

The beauty
of trees – turns out she loved them
more than me.

Opening the window
to let in the cool breeze –
horsefly.

Mossy lime kiln
rises like a Mayan ruin
from Robe Canyon.

Before picking peonies,
wind
picks them for me.

Gathered for supper –
a fly wrings its hands
in prayer.

How excited
the kitten to test
its new claws!

Such balance –
lady bug on the stone Buddha's
nose.

Rain-soaked,
seabirds are content to simply
bob upon the sea...

After the forest fire,
for the longest time –
no night songs.

Autumn winds
carry away
remnants of summer.

Such innocence,
the boy who asked –
"Who owns the moon?"

This priest
like a duck – lifting flock
to winter sky.

A red dragonfly
dances its way up
a rainbow...

Strolling the beach
at night – harvest moon hiding
amongst bunch grass.

At the marina,
floating
harbor seal carcass.

A dream of
the south – crepe myrtle
& kudzu.

At the gas pump,
running a dripping squeegee
over bugs on the windshield.

Cheap motel –
nightstand by the bed scarred
with cigarette burns.

Fading into sleep –
gentle patter of rain
upon the roof...

High tide,
path around the island –
gone.

A blue butterfly
& red dragonfly
day.

Old beach house –
has taken its share of beatings
from the ocean.

Do not the Salmon People
dwell in longhouses
beneath Salish Sea?

It was migrating salmon
who brought
moon & yellow salmonberries.

Bumblebee said,
"Weave your baskets quickly;
berries will ripen soon."

From spruce roots
& inner bark of cedar, she weaves
her baskets.

A woman of the earth –
she was buried
with her digging stick.

Look to blooming
Western dogwood to know
butter clams are ripe.

Did not People
of the River sing salmon upstream
to spawn?

First People
brought forth fern fiddleheads,
horsetail roots, salmonberry roots.

April
& the alders red with
swelling buds.

She paints
herself with vermilion –
the color of life.

Leave it to the voice's
of frogs
to signal winter's end.

It was rumored
she constantly lived beneath
a rain shadow.

Where the girl died,
wooden cross & teddy bear
by the road.

Kitten –
pouncing upon sun spots
on the living room carpet.

Beetle –
content to bask in a ray
of sunshine...

Through the mist,
bullfrog's "good morning" song
from the mill pond...

Grasshopper teeters
on the tip
of a blade of grass.

Sometimes breakfast,
the perfect way
to end a day!

Still amusing –
hummingbirds perched upon
blooming Crocosmia.

She said,
"There is hope in the blue iris's
blooming."

Abandoned birdhouse –
where spider
has made his home.

Life lesson –
child takes a stick to hive; bees take
their stingers to child.

"Is it time for feeding?"
ask circling koi,
fallen cherry blossoms.

Spring morning,
can't help but smile –
chirping birds...

Woman strolling baby
down sidewalk – tiny hand reaches
for clouds.

Tell me,
where would evolution be
without extinction?

He said,
"You live long enough, you'll find
your philosophy."

The weathered birdhouse,
no birds
have occupied for years.

Tonight –
how calm the stars,
how angry the sea.

Such a smile
upon face of boy
whale watching!

Spring morning –
rhubarb & strawberry inching
toward ripeness.

Hiking the
dark forest – owl lets me know
he's there.

Nightfall –
three crows on hemlock limb
share the day's adventures...

"Ha! Ha!"
Through the open pet shop doors,
parrot.

Six workers
in neon green vests standing
by a telephone pole.

By the railway station,
boy watches
trains pass by...

In the distance,
rising from the fog –
Hat Island.

That guitarist,
who lost a finger –
still playing.

Saturday morning –
cheers from the 14th hole
of the golf course.

It was after moving
from city to country,
I met dragonfly.

That boy
playing sheriff – how bright the star
on his denim shirt.

At the beach,
rustling grass from
salt, sea breeze...

Passing through the kitchen –
a fly
flies into me.

August evening –
prodigal hummingbird returns
to my feeder.

80 degrees –
overweight neighbor jogs down street
in gray sweats...

Girl on bike –
wears a helmet,
no shoes.

Rather than tattoos,
she adorned herself with
Autumn Meadowhawks.

That sailor –
such calloused hands
& tongue.

Between
gray sea & gray sky,
gray gull.

Approaching the terminal,
ferry
silently glides toward dock...

July afternoon –
dandelions litter the high school
football field.

Peeking from atop
Weeping Japanese maple –
Varied thrush.

A narcissist –
he dedicated the poem
to himself.

Just enough parting
of clouds
for sun to shine through.

Asked
why he runs, his reply –
"For sanity."

Sweltering day –
nothing but orange popsicles
in the freezer.

How curious
blue dragonfly hovering
above my kayak.

Sunday afternoon –
old man in his front yard napping
in a lawn chair.

Sometimes fog
settles so thick, there's no seeing
tomorrow.

How excited three-year-old
to see
his brother's bus off to school!

By my koi pond,
resting on sculpted heron's neck –
sparrow.

How gently
evening breeze carries loon's song
across mill pond...

Even now,
I still climb trees
just to do it.

Such a beautiful day –
even the birds
are smiling!

Girl in convertible –
drives down the road
singing loudly...

The child said
of the bagpiper – "Is he
killing a goose?"

The old house –
overgrown
with memories.

Writer –
"Sometimes I get in my car, let road
carry me where it will."

Do you wish to be
a leader? Listen closely to howl
of alpha wolf.

Netting leaves
from koi pond – whirr of hummingbird
overhead...

Mischievous cat –
the broken
potted plant.

To the Civil War
battlefield, the child brings
his toy soldiers.

Autumn wind
& with it – last remnants
of summer.

Such bright stars –
this
jasmine-scented evening.

Thrush is first
to arrive at my freshly-potted
strawberry pot.

Beneath the
blossoming cherry –
dead crow.

The frog leaps
into the koi pond without
a sound.

Leaving them
in the hot car – my yogurt pretzels
melt.

He searched
his whole life for the perfect wife
he never found.

Another spring day,
sun rises,
robin begins to sing...

Where the maple
once stood – a spot
of sunlight.

Past midnight –
neighbor cat's caterwauls
awaken me.

How straight
the old man walks
when drunk.

Childhood –
the sprinkler good for more
than watering lawns.

Sweltering afternoon,
my cell phone reads – "Needs to
cool down."

She traipses through
the universe;
no looking back.

Aged plum tree –
years have outlasted
blossoms.

Does not the future
of our world rest upon bones
of the past?

Just look
at those crows – trying to outfly
a jumbo jet!

Saturday morning –
planting strawberries in pots,
sun upon my back.

Picking mushrooms –
how easily she discerns between
good & bad.

Grandmother –
often she hummed while
she sewed.

On days when
the sea rages, she
rages too.

So many songs
about those brave, fallen warriors
of the past.

That bully –
always picking on the same
little boy.

Ripe strawberries –
tempting treats for the gathering
birds too.

And now she's dead –
I regret
words never said.

Autumn,
but girl skipping down sidewalk
singing summer songs...

Absent-minded professor –
thinking too little,
or too much?

At the party,
crowded room of familiar
strangers.

The old high school –
where gym showers haven't been used
for years.

I have no problem
with your existence, spider,
just – not in my house!

Every party –
he guards
the punchbowl.

Spring morning –
into a crystal vase she places
pink peonies.

Saturday morning –
neighbor dog barks, my cat stirs
in her sleep...

Where children
played on the sidewalk –
popsicle puddle.

Pompeii remains,
though – its ghosts
have fled.

Because she has
no children, widow next door
raises flowers.

That girl –
so much sassiness
in a small package!

Stepping into backyard
this morning – robin greets me
with song...

Autumn breeze –
leaves on my maple have taken
to sky.

Dragonfly summer –
that year I turned thirteen,
first noticed girls.

Such a shame –
that weeds should be
his garden claim.

The roof leaks –
a cooking pot gathers raindrops
in the kitchen...

Away, away,
that boy who from the meadow
strayed.

Flowering peonies –
just as beautiful
in moonlight.

After picking,
strawberry plants are blossoming
again!

Beneath these ancient bones,
flint arrowhead
from the Woodland period.

No birds
at my feeders this morning –
slinking neighbor's cat...

Child calling
to
a passing yellow butterfly...

At the train station,
homeward bound
& homeless.

No hummingbirds
at my nectar feeder, just –
bumble bee.

Giggling boy –
points to hovering
Blue Dasher dragonfly...

Some stars,
though distant, radiate
their joy!

Windy day –
her perfume wafting down
the sidewalk...

Regardless the weather,
mom & dad on the front porch
waving good-bye.

Where have all
the neighborhood rabbits gone –
predatory cat.

Setting sun –
from somewhere in the distance,
coyote's song.

Not sure
what to do next – boy atop
high dive at lake.

How funny –
crow chased from my feeder
by a sparrow!

That war general –
lives best
through his legends.

She said,
"You've got to stop defining yourself
through other people."

Sometimes she works
her body, simply to strengthen
her mind.

Regardless the season,
your smile carries the warmth
of sun, love.

What would
the firefly be without
his fire?

Both joy & sorrow –
know no
particular class of people.

How green the grass
where Civil War soldiers died
at Antietam.

How silently
she passed through this world
& into the next.

Old woman –
goes through her day thinking
about the past...

Arrival of summer –
how reluctant mountain
to give up its snow.

Look –
where the rainbow touched down,
flowering peonies!

Get out of the road,
crow,
I'm trying to drive!

How persistently
English lavender clings
to summer.

Yes, I'm a mathematician,
these syllables,
sometimes – 5-7-5.

Above the sea,
moon orchestrates
its mystery.

How natural it looks –
crimson yarrow
in an island garden.

Full moon
above mill pond – loon's song
beyond reed grass…

Waking from a night
on the street, homeless man
combs his hair.

Stoplight –
everyone glancing at the knock-out girl
in the crosswalk.

Dawn –
squirrel on the neighbor's roof
picking through moss.

July morning –
bees buzzing amongst
English lavender...

Amongst rocks
at the beach – Strongbow Apple
Cider cap..

Opening my mouth
to speak – spider's web on tip
of my tongue.

Spring –
old man smiling at pretty girls
in sundresses.

Cherry tree
struck by lightning, but –
still bearing fruit!

August morning –
fog blanketing the tips
of cornstalks.

All that's left
of the old mill – protruding pilings
in the river.

If you are quiet
& listen closely, earth reveals
its secrets.

Gray, rainy day –
eagle on his fir snag perch
anyway.

Who is your leader,
geese,
circling & circling gray sky...

The strawberry fields
of my youth – plowed under
for a shopping mall.

October morning –
mist in the limbs
of Douglas fir.

August –
farmer's rusty pickup abandoned
in pasture grass.

One week –
that's all it took for birds
to empty my feeder!

Passing cemetery –
military
honor guard at gravesite.

Beyond the distant
copse of trees, glimpse of
Stillaguamish River.

There –
in the dragonfly's eye,
sunlight.

On the floor
of the Honey Bucket,
cigarette butt.

Summer morning –
sunflower soaking up
falling rain.

That first year
teacher,
such – enthusiasm!

So many dogs
in the park, walking
their people.

Where sky
meets sea, & everywhere
in-between – fog.

Grandma always said,
"The greener Gravensteins make
the best pies."

Old tabby cat –
sleeps in the garden,
leaves birds alone.

Winter's bleakness,
crows scavenging –
scarecrow's blood.

Small town,
but up on the hillside –
large cemetery.

Leaf floating
atop koi pond – I thought
a dead fish.

For mental health,
I tend the garden a bit
every day.

She'd frequent beach
& look for starfish
to toss back into sea.

Beach sign –
"It's summer &
time for wandering."

What is it 'bout guys
in big trucks –
run you right off the road!

Autumn –
maple leaves dancing
down the street...

Homeless man
leaves 7-Eleven with – nothing
but a Lotto ticket.

Her social life –
postings
on Facebook.

First Communion –
gifted a black-bead rosary
from my Irish grandma.

As for me,
I do my best thinking
by the sea.

Midnight –
full snow moon, coyote's
howl…

He wandered the wasteland
with nothing but
vultures for company.

Driving to work –
a deer leaps onto the speedway,
halts traffic.

Saturday night –
Pizza Hut truck outside
the neighbor's house.

Ok,
who ate the flowers off
my crimson yarrow?

Driving through
South Carolina, humming
antebellum tunes...

Dusk –
she sits on porch swing, listens to
soft-falling spring rain...

He said,
"I even brake
for squirrels."

Mondays –
old harriers gathered on high school track
for a workout.

How like sparrow's song,
that
cross street push button.

By mailbox,
toddler in diapers on
wooden scooter.

His samurai sword,
so sharp –
it split dragonflies.

That garden gate –
leads to
a sticker patch.

Storm coming –
murder of crows passing
across brooding sky...

In the park,
puddle of seed where
pigeons feed.

Forgotten meadow –
but for
an empty railway wagon.

Abandoned trestle –
not good for much
but jumping into river.

She said,
"Your poetry consumes you;
& – me too."

What good the poet
without a little tragedy
in their life?

That poet –
how easily he forgets the days
when he's writing.

Every now & then,
in moments of loneliness –
coyote's howl.

How the booming canons
loosen
moisture from the clouds.

Far off,
to see the lightning, but –
never hear the thunder.

Lady & her dog,
strolling down the sidewalk –
both pregnant.

He said
"I love to write poetry; can't stand
listening to it!"

Because she slept
with wolves, she became
a wolf herself.

All that's left
of his coaching days – a whistle
& stop watch.

Pete, Sam, Bob,
three hoboes in the park –
trilogy or trinity?

Spring
& the homeless man –
smiling...

Garden owies –
typically look worse
than they are.

Through the yard,
blue dragonfly carrying
red lady bug.

In the pioneer cemetery,
robin on headstone
in full-throated song...

This year's marionberries –
nothing
but vines, few berries.

Where the horses have been,
everywhere –
road apples.

Sunset –
squadron of lady bugs
above mill pond.

That girl running –
how effortlessly she glides
across the land!

She said,
"When I contemplate a poem,
I listen to arabesques."

August –
forgotten gravestone
in flowered meadow.

Some Bigfoot
believers
never give up!

75th Anniversary of D-Day –
300 vets
gather at Normandy.

Getting up
to go to the bathroom – spooked by
a moon shadow!

Sunday afternoon –
waves rolling in & out, my grandkids
play on the beach...

Beyond the curve
of Earth, moon offers
its welcome.

Old bald eagle,
how aged his feathers, but – proudly
he holds his head.

Amongst the staked
campaign signs –
Mole Removal.

So much my child
has outgrown; but not her joy
of dragonflies.

Rich man & beggar man –
are they not
both forms of existence?

Midnight –
old man reading his Bible
by moonlight.

Walking sandy beach –
brightness of sun,
shrillness of gull's song.

Do flowering peonies
in the garden really need
a crystal vase?

Even now, retired general
wears
his sword in the garden.

Waking this morning –
first pangs
of mortality.

Something has gifted me
a cherry pit
on the birdfeeder.

The old man's
rowboat, now –
a flower garden.

The Paddle-tailed Darner
dragonfly –
"Mr. Happy Face"!

Autumn afternoon –
crow drinks from the edge
of my koi pond…

House floods –
husband upset, wife
redecorating.

Dawn –
from somewhere in my dream,
owl's hoot...

Spring morning,
can't help but smile –
chirping birds.

Dawn –
homeless man pushes shopping cart
down street...

Before her,
was there really
a me?

Crow at
my suet feeder, sees me approaching –
flies away.

His prized koi
floating atop pond –
no insurance.

Ah, to have
the metabolism of
a hummingbird!

Autumn morning –
crow in the neighbor's
birdbath.

On his nightstand,
a Bible
he's never read.

Mother's Alzheimer's,
yet – how she remembers ripened
Granny apples.

Waking this morning,
how lovely –
lavender in bloom.

That crow
on the neighbor's roof –
What's he pecking at?

Warm mornings –
she wears nothing in the garden
but a smile.

That dragonfly –
see how closely it resembles
a bi-plane!

The fly I let outside,
thanked me
by flying back inside!

Above the treetops,
in a wisp of billowy cloud –
crescent moon.

Night rafting
down the Deschutes River – so this is where
the stars gather!

Tell me,
does the hummingbird know
old age?

After mating,
how protective male dragonfly
of his female.

Fertilizing the lawn –
how healthy
the dandelions!

The old man's house,
I drove past on my way to work
for years – dark.

At stoplight,
girl in car beside me listening
to Zydeco music...

Driving past the latte stand
to catch
a glimpse of bikini baristas!

In the lap
of stone Buddha,
black beetle.

After the rain,
robins
scavenging in the garden.

Retirement,
his first task – shut off
the alarm clock.

Sometimes,
even on her happy days –
rain.

At the beach,
child asks – "Where are all
the baby gulls?"

In the neighbor's garden,
ivy has
a will of its own.

Dawn –
black-booted crow trudges across
neighbor's roof...

Hard to gaze
at moon's beauty with her beauty
so near.

Into the lake
dragonfly splashes to cleanse
its self.

Sometimes angry,
sometimes calm, sea has
its temperaments too.

Old man –
still chases butterflies
in his mind's eye.

Sudden breeze –
rush of waves against
the beach...

Dawn –
gray heron stalks through
the tidal flats...

Small town,
how quiet, but for the
passing train...

Something 'bout
that distant island, keeps –
calling...

Sailboat passes –
old man on beach
silently watches...

Bad as things were,
he went
back to her.

Virginia night –
watching fireflies flit above
distant meadow...

August afternoon,
tending garden – shadow
of dragonfly.

Headed to baseball –
mom's station wagon full
of Little Leaguers.

Let me live
in remote places, closer to animals
than man.

When bad
things happen – he writes
poems.

Summer's end –
cutting back
the yellow daisies.

August morning –
waking early to catch the
Perseid meteor shower.

She wonders –
"Will my life story ever have
a happy ending?"

Don't tell me you've outgrown
the meadow
where we played as children.

Driving –
duck makes me swerve around him
in the road.

Hiking –
how clear & cold water
from mountain stream.

Atop lights
in the old stadium,
osprey's nest.

Late spring –
caterpillar gnaws
on an apple leaf.

He carries Jesus
on one should, Buddha
on the other.

Gardening after dark –
harvest moon
as my lantern.

Some mornings –
easier to write haiku
than make the bed!

Father advice –
"Someday when you retire,
go quietly."

After the rain,
Crocosmia glistening
in sunlight.

She knows it all –
moon,
stars & beyond.

So, this is my reward
for picking blackberries –
thorn in thumb!

Pretty swift –
that boy who chased down
dragonfly.

After all these years,
still – I've
never seen an old butterfly.

Birds at my feeder,
& through the shrubs – slinking
neighbor's cat...

Spring garden –
bountiful with flowers
& weeds.

Hard to top
the music
of Mother Nature!

Walking the neighborhood
at dusk – dog barks
from the neighbor's house...

She said,
"I smoke pot for
medicinal purposes."

Sudden breeze –
afternoon aflutter with
cherry blossoms...

Driving the highway –
"Get out of the road, crow!
Get out of the road!"

Winter –
old man holds a picture
of himself as a boy.

The old man said,
"I don't have much; but, what I do have
is enough."

Walking through town –
child hums a nursery rhyme
from my childhood…

To the girl
with the wicked tongue –
"No potty mouth!"

Was it butterfly
who rang
the temple bell?

Silvery drops of rain
puddling
on a fallen maple leaf.

August afternoon –
cows graze
in the shade of trees.

Long line of autos
slowly passing
scavenging crow in road...

Fetching the paper,
I awaken owl who lets me know
he's annoyed.

Nothing but stories
to remember the fallen soldier's
glory.

How gently
the girl cradles Eight-Spotted
Skimmer dragonfly.

Once again,
east of the Cascades – sun,
west of the Cascades – rain.

Homeless man
beneath an umbrella – such
sad eyes.

Tending garden –
startled by a stick
mistaken for a snake!

The old parrot –
more observing than talking
these days.

Is it true,
the dragonfly's favorite meal –
mosquitoes?

Sweltering afternoon –
long line
at Joe's popsicle truck.

Sick in bed –
June sun high
in the sky.

Blackie Spit –
where migrating birds gather
to discuss the weather.

Bit by a spider –
to scratch
or call Poison Control?

Since the farmhouse burned,
they've moved
into the barn.

Spider drifting
across lake on web – catches
a dragonfly.

Peaking from behind
rhododendron –
Black-eyed Susan.

Autumn wind
with its subtle hints –
winter's coming...

Cardinal Meadowhawk
dips into lake,
lays a few eggs.

The neighbor's dog
has trampled my Crocosmia
again!

Birds-of-Paradise
with a slight breeze –
they fly too!

The wind has passed –
crows emerge
from limbs of Douglas fir.

Just past midnight
in the "No Fireworks" neighborhood –
fireworks!

Who knew –
the sumo wrestler does
Sumi-e brushstroke too!

How willingly
those cattle follow one another
to slaughter.

At the ranger station,
flash of lightning & - eyes turn
to forest.

Every wish
she ever makes – sign
of the cross.

Sunday morning
with –
the Zumba Zombies!

Pouring wine –
I lick a drop from top
of bottle.

Talk about
making my day – girl in bikini
on roller skates!

Such a mountain climber –
ant making his way
up a granite boulder.

Nothing else to do –
crows taunt
a Barred owl.

So calm
sea & sky – one sheet
of blue.

That nature poet –
such a deep love for
Mother Earth.

Winter –
grandpa's hound at foot of bed
keeping his feet warm.

A calm sea –
perfect for crossing
the bar.

Something about
dew & spider webs amongst
wildflowers.

Practicing tai chi –
snow flake lands on old man's
outstretched finger.

Such a knockout,
that girl in the "Mama Llama"
t-shirt!

German Shepard
emerges from lake – smile
on his face.

By the lake,
two poles fishing without
a fisherman.

By the
autumn lake, old man
practicing tai chi.

In the park,
empty wooden bench, leaning
madrone.

That girl
on the park bench – reading
Sylvia Plath.

Jogging around
Green Lake – dodging
goose poop.

Waking this morning –
Is it
Friday or Saturday?

Ah, to
wake up thinking
poetry!

A broken heart –
he's become a rudderless ship
at sea.

Squirrel who frolicked
in the neighborhood –
dead in the road.

Zipping through
the alley –
old man on motor scooter.

Boy on bike –
keeping right up
with traffic!

Latte stand barista,
now –
an elementary school teacher.

Migrant worker's
roadside fruit stand –
"Fresh Cherries".

A second too late –
frog leaping at
passing dragonfly.

Sunny day –
horsefly basking on
my shingled roof.

Jogger –
chugging down the road
& texting!

Abandoned driftwood
beach hut –
occupied by crows.

Portion of beach
for everyone – kids, lovers,
Great blue heron.

Sandy spit,
low tide,
beached sailboat.

That boy –
always feeling the need
to prove himself.

Where Indians,
Japanese, loggers, soldiers dwelt –
ferry terminal.

Great-horned owl flying
with
an escort of crows...

Dawn –
three crows chase Barred owl
from neighbor's roof.

Old bee –
still buzzing, minus
a couple "z's".

Old dog –
doesn't leave porch, but offers
a weak, protective bark.

Some politicians –
more crooked
than the crooks!

Because his father
was a lawyer, he became
a lawyer too.

The house they built
outlasted
the marriage.

That farmer –
such
a love for the land.

He plowed under
his corn –
started growing pot.

That native
dancer – dancing back
his ancestors...

The old farmer said,
"You must
keep this land going."

How talented
dragonfly whisperer – whispering to
a deaf insect!

Yes, even dragonflies
have their
favorite perches.

To be a leader
& not lose sight of
one's humanity.

That damselfly –
I mistook
for a dragonfly.

She said,
"If you're going to take a photo,
include people."

Neighbor boy –
practicing his batting skills
on my daisies.

Just for laughs –
black lab chases floating gulls
further out to sea.

July
& – the world teaming
with blueberries!

Dusk –
how far cedar limb bends
under crow's weight.

She was at her best
with
an empty nest.

Sunny day –
hawk navigates an ocean
of blue.

The list of dragonflies –
long as
a summer day.

The blooming
English lavender – she's
a child again!

Blue Dasher –
how swiftly you elude the boy's
dragonfly net!

Sweltering day –
dog gets a lick of the child's
ice cream cone.

Old hermit
who lives in a cave – quite happy without
electric bills.

Only one on
main street of town tonight –
firefly.

Sunrise –
How enthusiastically
parakeet sings!

A warning
from my daughter – "Never get between our dog
& its bone."

A tree has fallen –
it hit the one house in town
without insurance!

How funny –
sparrow chasing koi
around the pond!

Eventually, Raven
perched in Douglas fir
becomes – night.

Winter storm –
oak scratches its protests against
my window.

Beyond farmhouse,
poplars dancing in the wind,
except for one.

Across the sky,
plane, disappearing in & out
of clouds…

Evening breeze –
ah, the neighbors are barbecuing
salmon again.

My granddaughter
yells, "Gramps, watch this!"
does a cartwheel.

Sunday,
2:00 a.m., the city still not ready
to go to sleep.

That photo
of great-great grandpa – looks like
it was taken yesterday!

All summer,
how patiently she waits
for her garden stew.

Tell me, robin,
are you puffed in song,
or against the cold?

That dragonfly
I whispered onto my finger –
fell asleep.

The font used for this book is Cambria. Cambria is a serif typeface ommissioned by Microsoft. It was designed by Dutch typeface designer Jelle Bosma in 2004. Because of its very even spacing and proportions, Cambria appears very readable when printed at small sizes. This serf font is a registered trademark of the Microsoft Corporation in the United States.

CPSIA information can be obtained
at www.ICGtesting.com
Printed in the USA
LVHW031143141019
634125LV00002B/522/P